OVERWHELMED US

TARUN (KEN)

Made with ♥ on the Notion Press Platform
www.notionpress.com

For her, who tried her very best not to be worst.

And for him, who made sure we never see her at her worst.....

Contents

Contents

Preface

Him who was lost saw an hope and drowned deep in his thoughts....
submerged with sorrow, Overwhelmed by the feeling of hollowness
To push this feeling of being Empty, He started writting about the things
he felt, To see if there is someone like him, Someone who was lost to....

Acknowledgements

- I'm eternally grateful to my Tau Ji (Uncle), Davinder Rana. Who motivated me alot. He taught me discipline, tough love, manners, respect, and so much more that will help me to succeed in life. I truly have no idea where I'd be if he wasn't with me...
- To all the individuals I have had the opportunity to lead, be led by, or watch their leadership from afar, I want to say thank you for being the inspiration.

Foreword

Dear readers,

It feels strange for me to write these words, as I committed to never write forewords.

I'm making a rare exception. First, this verse novels is sympathetic for me. Second, Tarun

is my great friend. Third, I want this types of book in market so individuals will relate and see

that they aren't the only one to face this emotions in there life

Prologue

You are as rare as MOON,

- **Its not even our love story that I miss, Its the friendship we used to have..**
- **206 bones in my body, And yet you chose to break the one part of me I'd never be able to fix..**
- **It started like it ended, As strangers**
- **At the end I dont know what ended, Our story or me.**
- **THANK YOU FOR EVERYTHING MY BELOVED!**

1. I HOPE

Everything
I wonder what you see ,
when we're sitting next to each other in the closest possible manner
and you look at me
Do you see something surreal, sublime and new?
Or you see just another dream, that we cannot make true?
Does it feel like your finest childhood days?
birthday dresses , late night ice-creams, all the cultural dances and plays... dancing while staring in each other eyes
And I don't surely know what you see but I hope I you see a friend , a soul for your soul
a place to keep your heart safe and sound for life
for life , a place that makes you feel like home a place u feel u can put ur face on my chest & cry till u want & i'll pat ur head tell u that its okay m here m ryt here just see me reach me nothing in return just ur attention just ur care
I hope u'll understand me
I hope u'll kill that darkness of mah thoughts.....

2. YOU

My favourite music has always been Sad
and my favorite time of day has always been night,
So i find it almost ironic that i fell in love with you,
The brightest person i ever met.
I have always be attached to the moon and the darkness that surrounds it.
But you make me want to love the moon and i that may have something to do with the fact that you are my MOON....

3. HE WISHES THE MOON

I wish u can try i wish u can reach that deepness of my thoughts i wish you'll be the one who'll truly understand me i wish you'll value me i wish you'll know me i wish just an wish & wishes are imposible to come true....So its my fault.....

Oh, well the world is dreaming
Under the May moon,
His soul in love with moon..
His senses all a-swoon...
Everyone is sleeping but he...
Staring at moon like an owl trying to understand his feelings trying to hold the moon atleast once in his arms trying to just reach that moon one day....

4. KNOWING OURSELVES

He was standing on bridge
With null mind & half ded soul,
Pushed by the fellings deep inside his heart
Its all dark covered by the layers of sorrow.
He wish an light like the moon,
Which show hope during black nights reach him one day & help him with all his anxiety & overthinking the fear of his ownself.
He trying to know himself
He trying to get rid of that social anxiety but somewhere he knows that this anxiety is his real friend overthinking is his "HOPE", Seeing moon & sky for hours at night help him little bit to undertstand his thoughts & feel calm for a while.
An unhappy heart is like strained eyes even the wind hurts?

5. TO BE WITH YOU

I've had this urge to draw you ,
Cause I was too afraid to ask you from destiny ;
So I thought making a portrait ,
Was the only way to keep you with me.
But I'm not really good with colors ,
You can't have a way with everything right ;
And people can call me a fool for all the decisions I make ,
But I'd never risk depicting such a heavenly sight.
So I paint you with words everyday ,
I use melted rainbows to replicate the tint of your eyes
Knowing that nothing can ever match the depth of your heart ,
I end up turning to those infinite night skies.
Which never ends with sunrise......

6. APOCALYPES AND WE

Apocalypse and us
What if the sky ever crumbles ,
And the ocean goes out of control?
Would we still find each other ,
And swim together to the shore?
What if the stars break into pieces ,
And shoot down from the aether?
Would we still hold hands ,
And make a wish to be together?
Well some things are better left unsaid ,
Some thoughts are better left untold.
Maybe some things are better left unsaid ,
But i just wanna make sure you know.
That if the world really caves in ,
There's nothing else that I'd rather do.
Cause there isn't a better way to feel alive ,
Than to die next to you.
We'd climb up a burning building
To see the apocalypse from the roof ,
And if everyone below would watch us
I'd still love to kiss you.

7. HIM & HER

HER:-
All I know is ,
when I look at the empty sky , I see
freedom racing
when I see empty faces I see stories , stories that are often left untold
secrets in the ocean , serenity in the moon
And all I know is that I see them all , everything at once ;
When I look at you.
HIM:-
All you know is nothing but a precious peice of living..
The sky isn't empty there is stars shining like they are best but deep inside they going through alot unable to share unable to talk just to pretend that they fine, We wanna discover that ocean the ocean where all your treasure are trapped. Whenever we meet I just dont know whats it but it's something i wanna know....

8. MAYBE

Portraying your hair with golden rain ,
Your hug with a green limitless meadow
A home for the comfort that you give
And sunshine for your beauty and glow.
I knit our lives together with a pen
Quoting that we're meant to be ,
Aware of all the differences we have
I still paint us as a perfect harmony.
I fancy delivering these letters that my soul wrote for you ,
Maybe cause your reply makes me feel as if you're really mine ;
Maybe because I like being the reason behind that happiness ,
Or maybe just because I love seeing that smile maybe i just wanna hug u maybe i just wanna hold u tight & gaze in ur eyes maybe i just wanna talk whole day with u maybe i just need ur existence maybe i wanna cook food for u maybe i wanna play guitar with u,

Maybe & for sure i wanna love u like u never felt ?

9. DESIRE

Being listened & heard is greatest desire of human heart it's a story about the Sun loving the Moon. On a more deep level it's a story about the sacrifices that each of them maybe be asked to make throughout our lives...ITS CALLED AN "ECLIPSE" THE eclipse of all our happiness "don't you dare to abandon your blessing of light for my darkness for my anxiety which has stayed with me for years & they r my hope?

I know there is no any match for SUN & MOON!

10. LEMME KNOW

It hurts sometime it makes us happy lets think positive lets smile once more lets take a break & understand eachother why we have to wait for rain to stop lets go in rain & dance while gazing in eachother eyes lets enjoy the rain every drop is Lucky that it got a chance to feel your presence lets run lets run together to the end just us knowing eachother lemme adore u lemme appreciate u lemme know u lemme reach the darkness inside u & lemme be the hope to show u right path to the future u deserve to the happiness u deserve everything ? lets smile lets survive

11. I WANNA

Right now, I'm in a state of mind
I wanna be in like all the time;
Ain't got no tears left to cry.
I wanna get ill ...
I wanna get die...
I wanna get ill...
I wanna get diee...
I have seen enough
I dont wanna survive...
I just wanna walk mile with you..
& you just shredded that dream with a smile...

12. DESTINED END

When my heart could no longer illuminate, I gazed towards horizons shrouded in blurry blackness revealing the agony of my sorrows to the moon. Wondering if it would, wondering if that moon seeing me thoo...what is life ehhh???? Why wanna survive????

Life is not an empty dream!
For the soul is dead that slumbers,
And things are not what they seem.
Life is real! Life is earnest!
And the words was not said by the soul.
Not enjoyment, and not sorrow,
Is our destined end or way

13. BUSY TO REALIZE

They say happiness will find you,
But I think sadness will find you too,
It sneaks up on you in darkness,
Just when you think you've made it through,
It opens holes in what was solid ground,
The kind you never know are there,
Until you go to take another step,
And find you're standing over the air,
The world around you passes by,
In blurs of colour and sound,
Nothing around you making sense,
As you continue your plummet down,
You can't remember how it started,
And you don't know when it will end,
But you know that you'd give anything,
To stand up on your feet again,
Sadness is that feeling,
When the falling doesn't stop,
And it saps your life of meaning,
And of the good things that you've got,
So when you finally hit rock bottom,
And you look back up at the sky,
What you once had seems so far away,
The only thing left to do is cry,
People all yell out "save yourself",

Calling things about "happiness" and "hope".But they're too busy with their lives to realise....

Overwhelmed Us

Today, I felt something unusual,
Something new, That had became old
The sparks I once had
Are GONE the smile is GONE

Overwhelmed Us

And If I ever hear our song again,
A smile will, Without doubt bloom on
my face. Only to die the way our love did:
Gradually but Beautifull<3

Overwhelmed Us

His name was engraved in her heart,
But not in her destiny.
And He was her most beautifull unfulfilled wish....

Overwhelmed Us

I'll find you again in next life and
make "US" last.

I may have turned the page,
But half of my soul will always be the bookmark to your chapter..

Overwhelmed Us

"YOU WERE MY PEACE,
NOW YOU ARE THE CAUSE OF MY CHAOS"

Overwhelmed Us

"WRONG NUMBER" said a familiar voice.
But even after all of that you'll still be my
favourite Incomplete wish....

Overwhelmed Us

Someone asked me do I know you,
Million thoughts rolled my mind.
But I just said "NO".

Overwhelmed Us

We knew togetherness shall
    end one day, Death hoped would be
    the reason but yet here we are.
    Alive and Separate....

Overwhelmed Us

I believe that our love was sand,
It kept slipping out of hands.
Because how could something so perfect
from the beginning, Start to feel like a Burden

Overwhelmed Us

AND MAYBE ONEDAY,
  MAYBE JUST ONE MORE TIME;
  OUR LOVE WILL REUNITE ONCE AGAIN

Printed by Libri Plureos GmbH in Hamburg,
Germany